PERSONAL EFFECTIVENESS

for the

SYSTEMS MAN

HE5500
.M364

From the Systemation Letter

Leslie H. Matthies

systemation, inc.

Box 730, Colorado Springs, Colo.

© 1968 by Leslie H. Matthies

Editor
William H. Marcus

Produced under direction of
The FOUNDATION for ADMINISTRATIVE RESEARCH
Box 730   Colorado Springs, Colo.

Printed in the United States of America

ABOUT THIS HANDBOOK

What is the prime requisite for you to be a top-flight systems man? What is the one characteristic that separates the systems pro from the systems technician?

"Well," you may say, "he's an expert in computers and programming languages . . . or in data collection and analysis . . . or in forms design . . . or in survey techniques . . . or in procedures development . . . or in etc., etc."

If your answer is similar to these, you're, at best, partly right. True, we find most systems men are technically competent in one or more of such systems specialties.

However, we've found that the real systems professional is the person who makes PEOPLE his first consideration when he starts a project. The professional man realizes that he can increase his own effectiveness only if he gains the cooperation and the respect of the line supervisors and operators who are *in* the system.

Like management, systems work is a people art. So, how do you become an artist in people work? Basically, it involves molding your attitude and your personality so that you become more sensitive to people's needs, feelings, and desires.

First, you must realize your own shortcomings. What is your ability now to relate to others? Once you've identified your weak spots, you can then make a conscious effort to overcome these deficiencies.

Are you a poor listener? Then concentrate on techniques that force you to really hear and understand what the other fellow is saying.

Do you know how to include your line people in your systems projects so that they know they're really making a significant contribution to systems improvement?

Do you know how to organize, coordinate, and

guide the efforts of the individuals on a project team . . . a team made up of systems "amateurs"? As the only pro, you must provide the leadership, you know.

How skilled are you at getting results without authority? Do you know how to be a leader without being a manager? Do you know how a systems man, without line authority, gains the cooperation of the various work groups in his organization?

We've designed this handbook as your guide to more personal effectiveness. We hope you'll use it often. As you strive to become a more effective member of your organization's management team, do remember that any improvement—even a small amount—is worthwhile.

CONTENTS

What Is The FOUNDATION
for ADMINISTRATIVE RESEARCH?

It is a nonprofit corporation, founded in 1959, with this job to do:

★ *To improve administration through systems*

FAR'S techniques are educational in nature. Its theme is "on-the-job application."

We don't educate a man who thinks he'd *like* to do systems work. We train him only while he is *doing* systems work.

In cooperation with administrators everywhere, FAR means to help by:

   ✔ 1. Identifying today's BEST administrative systems. This means discovery of the present outer boundaries of systems state-of-the-art.

   ✔ 2. Pushing planned research projects that go beyond the boundaries of our present systems knowledge.

   ✔ 3. Extracting the principles behind such systems.

   ✔ 4. Developing educational plans for passing successful principles on to people who will use them.

Like a more detailed account of the Foundation and its aims? Ask for the "FAR Booklet."

Write FAR, Box 730, Colorado Springs, Colo. 80901.

CHAPTER I

HOW EFFECTIVE ARE YOU?

How effective are you—as a systems worker?

Can you get a job done in the same time as the average systems worker? Or in *half* the time? Or do you take *twice* the amount of time that the average man would take?

Give conscious attention to your result-getting effectiveness. Ask:

> *How effective am I? Where do I rate on the scale from LEAST to MOST effective?*

Examine your personal working habits during the day. Four or five times during the day ask yourself:

> *Could I do THIS (whatever you're engaged in at the moment) better?*

SELF-SUPERVISION

As a systems worker you cannot be supervised in the usual sense. You have only one basic guide as you do systems work—that is to work as effectively as you can. You can become personally more effective if:

> 1. *You are willing to QUESTION your present effectiveness.*
> 2. *You're willing to seek, consciously, ways of becoming MORE effective.*

Thus you will have recognized your obligation to your organization . . . to provide, at the least cost, the improvements it needs within its various systems.

Your work is largely of an intangible nature. You don't turn out a "product" that the boss can see. So there is the opportunity to "goof-off" and to work at lower than top effectiveness . . . if you want to.

A man who wants to "fiddle around going through motions" instead of getting swift results, can get away with it for awhile. But not indefinitely.

His lack of results will be the signal, sooner or later, that he must be separated from his staff job. He must go back to a kind of work where a supervisor can "keep an eye on him."

THE PRICE TAG ON SYSTEMS RESULTS

How would a manager react if an auditor said to him:

> *You spent $600 worth of time to get a systems result that you could have had for $250!*

Any systems manager who has been operating a systems program knows that there is a wide-spread difference in the *effectiveness* of systems men.

Seldom do you get a chance to compare one systems worker to another.

One corporate systems manager, however, did get such a chance. The corporate controller asked him to clean up cumbersome petty cash purchasing systems in two different plants.

The systems man assigned to the job in plant A completed his work in 15 working days . . . 120 working hours. He earned about $5 an hour, so he used $600 worth of his time.

Another man carried out the same assignment in plant B. Yet he used only 50 hours. His pay rate was the same . . . about $5 an hour, so the cost here was $250.

The corporate systems director, struck by the $350 difference in time costs did a bit of investigating to see if the circumstances surrounding the two assignments were similar. He concluded that they *were* substantially the same.

EXPLAINING SYSTEMS VALUES

A few elements of systems improvements are measurable . . . and systems men do measure them. But we'd also like to provide convincing measurements on ALL aspects of systems improvement work.

To be effective on a continuous basis, the systems man must help the top boss see the value in systems benefits.

How do we explain, convincingly, systems values that aren't measurable? How do you measure the value of more adequate control? Or of superior teamwork? Easier data handling? Shorter transaction cycles? Or better service to your customers?

We KNOW there's solid value in such results. Yet such value doesn't lend itself to dollar and cents proof. So how do you "tell the value story"? How do you put the light on systems values so that men see them more clearly?

TOUGH EVALUATION

If the work output is *tangible* a top manager can decide whether it is worth its cost (in time and its equivalent in salary).

This is not true of systems results. Systems outputs are usually INtangible.

At least a portion of the systems man's effort to be effective must be concentrated on making clear to his top management what systems benefits they've received.

Failure in this facet of his staff effectiveness . . . can result in two tragic occurrences, both as a result of the inevitable economy waves that roll over any organization:

1. *A cut in payroll whereby the systems worker himself is laid off*
2. *An abrupt stoppage in the continuous effort toward better systems*

So a part of the systems man's total personal effectiveness must include reasonable skill in "salesmanship." Such a skill should help him translate systems benefits into terms of value that any manager will appreciate. —

JUGGLING MANY PROJECTS

The systems man who is confident of his ability to get results is not flustered when he must carry on a number of systems improvement jobs simultaneously.

His multiproject balancing act may consist of a major project with a number of subprojects.

The effective systems man can keep a number of projects going.

Or he may juggle a number of non related systems improvement jobs . . . yet keep all moving toward completion. Such a man is effective because:

> *Any time he is stopped by circumstances or by other people on one project, he turns his attention to another project.*

Some men find it very stimulating to be able to switch from one type of work to another.

Admittedly other men find it confusing.

But the more effective man is not phased by having to carry on a number of projects at one time.

How Effective Are You?   **9**

3 CLASSES OF SYSTEMS EFFECTIVENESS

Some systems people provide benefits with values that outweigh their own salaries from 3 to 10 times.

But there is the other kind, too, the kind of person who should be ashamed to accept his pay check.

You'll find this last type only in a poorly disciplined department where the systems manager is a "softie" and permits other executives to thrust on him men who cannot succeed in other areas.

In relation to his effectiveness you can classify the systems worker as:

> 1. *A man who doesn't TRY to do an effective job. He doesn't really CARE.*
> 2. *A man who tries to do a job, but DOES NOT KNOW HOW to get results quickly.*
> 3. *A man who gets results quickly because he TRIES and because he KNOWS HOW.*

Once you classify a man in the first category, scrape him off. Put him back into a job where he has a supervisor breathing down his neck. He is not a type of person who should be doing staff work.

The 2nd type, the man who *tries,* really *wants* to get a job done. Do not be hard on him. Help him. Provide him with some solid training.

To the 3rd type of man, give the rewards that he deserves . . . in salary . . . and in appreciation . . . and in challenges.

THE CREATIVITY PEAK

When the effective systems man develops, after much effort, the "just right" idea for a new system . . . other people see it as a relatively simple answer to the problem. They may say:

> *Why didn't we think of that before?*

People in the organization who do not do systems work are not aware of the process the effective systems man goes through to get that answer that looks

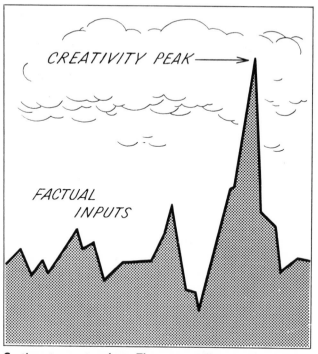

Continue to sweat and try. The answer will come as a pinnacle called the "creativity peak."

so easy.

One man, who had created a number of highly profitable ideas for his organization, was asked why he was so personally effective. He said:

> *I'm willing to sweat first . . . and I know that inspiration will come.*

Systems work can be hard, mule-work. A systems man often feels discouraged. He has his black moment when he feels:

> *I don't think I'll ever get the answer to this messy problem!*

But the professional also knows that if he keeps at it . . . if he continues to pour into his mind the

How Effective Are You? 11

factual inputs . . . if he continues to do the pick and shovel work like searching through files . . . or talking to people . . . or conducting personal interviews . . . or analyzing and puzzling over the data he secures . . . charting data and sorting the information . . . that the answer finally *will* come.

A MASTER OF TECHNIQUES

The effective systems man is a master of useful systems techniques. Whether he gains these through training or experience, each enables him to get results quickly. Here are a few of his techniques:

- [ ] 1. *He doesn't write, he TELEPHONES when practical.*
- [ ] 2. *He doesn't puzzle over a complex operation, he FLOW CHARTS it*
- [ ] 3. *He uses the PLAYSCRIPT procedure sequence to see what contribution people make who are "in the act."*
- [ ] 4. *He takes SAMPLES of time rather than makes a 100% study to find out about conditions*
- [ ] 5. *He PLANS before he acts*
- [ ] 6. *He spells out and knows the exact SYSTEMS FLOW and its path, before he starts to investigate it.*
- [ ] 7. *He writes a CLEAR ASSIGNMENT before he starts any kind of work*
- [ ] 8. *He DICTATES rather than scribbles.*
- [ ] 9. *He is always thinking about how other PEOPLE can give a hand.*

How many of these techniques do you use? There are, of course, other techniques that the effective systems man uses.

BACKGROUND AIDS EFFECTIVENESS

A systems man's background . . . his *experience*, his *knowledge*, his formal *education*, and his *contin-*

uing education . . . has a definite bearing on his effectiveness.

If a man's background is blank—if he has no knowledge of administration, of management processes, of office practices, or of systems techniques—he may be a very sincere worker but he is not likely to be effective.

By contrast, the man with a rich background of well-organized knowledge and experience, can be most effective in getting systems results . . . and in least amount of time.

To be effective, a man needs a rich systems/administrative background.

CHAPTER 2

USING TIME EFFECTIVELY

Our supply of time is always less than our supply of equipment, buildings, energy, money, skills, materials, or land.

It's easy to lose time . . . and not even be aware of the loss.

Money, particularly, we guard with great care. We guard other assets with reasonable care. Not so with time.

We seldom keep a record of the time we use or what we use it for. In a few cases, we do have some idea of the cost of time (in money only) because we can measure the productivity of a few workers.

In the case of an executive (or a staff man) we don't charge his time to any specific job.

Executive and staff time is an asset that flows by largely unguarded. So we suffer losses, substantial losses of time, simply because we permit our time to be wasted, misused, or frittered away.

☛ *In most cases we aren't aware of the loss.*

An executive, for instance, may waste time, not because he isn't working, but because he is working on the *wrong things*. He works on items that don't have a large payout.

His time is limited. If he uses it all on B class jobs, he must neglect A class activities that could have provided a large payout for his organization.

THE REAL COST OF LOST TIME

If an executive receives $80 a day and he works at only 50% of his effectiveness, what is the loss? $40 a day?

The loss from poor use of executive time is more serious than that. The loss is so serious it can affect the future of the organization . . . denying the organization investments in its future.

As many a small business manager has found (who struggled in a bewildered way to "keep things going") poor use of time can result in disaster.

First comes a *bankruptcy* of results . . . then service . . . then goods . . . and finally of money. The verdict: *poor management.* The real reason: *poor use of time.*

Of course we must have people in the organization today doing *today's* work. But the organization cannot remain healthy if no one looks ahead.

If the executive doesn't invest at least a portion of his time today on work that will get a result for the organization tomorrow, who else will do it?

Characteristics of Time. It flows by us swiftly. We can't store it. Each man's daily allotment of time is exactly the same as every other man's.

While we can't store time, it does permit *investment.* As time flows by us today, we can do something that will bring a desirable result tomorrow.

A man's results come from the manner in which he uses his time.

CHALLENGE ROUTINE

Identify work as executive work . . . or the other kind . . . routine.

If the work turns out to be something that a person does over and over . . . if it is on a regular schedule, or another person can be trained to do it . . . it IS routine.

True, it is work that must be done. But if the executive who is paid and trained to do other work does the routine kind, he "shortchanges" his organization. Executive work must be creative . . . never routine.

Here are two "feel" tests for *executive* as opposed to *routine* work:

☐ Does this work have an uncertain, risky, unsettled feeling? *It is probably executive work.*

☐ Does it have a sure feeling? Is it comfortable? Do you know exactly when you can finish it? *It is probably routine work.*

If you are a staff man or an executive, and you identify a job you're doing as routine, IT ISN'T YOUR WORK!

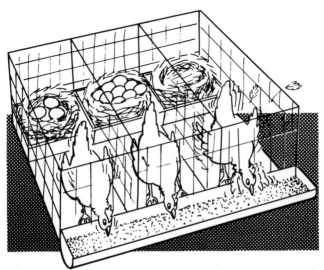

Fluttery, bush activity can consume time without getting a result.

Don't do it. It is somebody else's job. You can't afford to give your time to that work simply because there's no one else to do YOUR work.

In any healthy organization, the creative process must be continual. Improvements must be continual. The improved coordination process must be continuous. Planning must be continual. All these are executive/staff types of work.

A self-starter to creative work is the question:

What should I be doing NOW to help insure the future of my organization?

The executive who finds the answer to that question knows that he has started on and will continue to work on the creative process expected of executives.

MEASURE RESULTS AGAINST TIME USED

It is not the work, the project, or the job that counts. It is the *result* that counts. Focus on the (1) *result* and the (2) *time* it took to get that result.

If the total time is high, and the result seems low in value . . . won't you tend to abandon such effort?

By this thinking, you can decide whether you are spending too much time on the jobs of lesser importance.

Because you're conscious of your *work-time* ratio you'll spend more of your limited time on the jobs that stack up high in value.

GIVE SOME TIME TO TOMORROW

Today's problems press in on us and "insist" that we solve them. How many of those problems could have been solved far easier in the *past* if we hadn't ignored the *future*?

At least a share of executive time must go to a problem that isn't one yet.

The present is quick, noisy, and clamorous. The future is quiet, subtle, and slow. It will get none of your time, if you aren't alert.

Do-it-nowers want you to solve all of today's problems immediately.

If you're giving all your time "to putting out fires," to solving today's problems, who is taking the time to look ahead?

If from 25 to 30 percent of your time doesn't go to tomorrow, you're probably shortchanging your organization's future.

DECIDING ON THE VALUE OF EXECUTIVE JOBS

The trap many executives and their staff men fall into is to chew away on and "get out of the way" the jobs that somebody drops on their desks.

Yet the people who bring these jobs to the executive are not in a position to know the job's relative value to the organization. No matter how much pressure they may put on to get *their* jobs done, they can't judge the relative value of jobs.

One man, concerned about making better use of his time, worked out a simple rating technique that helps him.

Don't ignore the importance of investing some time in the future.

He gives each job a rating based on his own opinion of that job. The ratings are 3 . . . (1) the future value of the work, (2) the importance of the work, and (3) the timeliness of the work.

He recognizes that a share of his work (30% or more) must be of such a nature that it will have value *in the future.* Research, development, planning, forecasting, setting objectives, and setting up programs for developing executives . . . are all jobs that can bring valuable results in the future.

He divides all jobs that come to him into 3 groups, those that fall in the top 3rd, the middle 3rd, or the lower 3rd of importance. The position depends on how he rates the job in respect to its future value, its importance, and its timeliness. The following table gives an idea of his thinking:

	Future Value of the Work	*Importance of the Work*	*Timeliness of the Work*
Top 3rd	A	A	A
Middle 3rd	B	B	B
Lower 3rd	C	C	C

If upon a few minutes reflection, he rates the job C-C-C, a minor job, he refuses to do it. He immediately assigns it to a subordinate, to a staff man, or to his own secretary.

One of the jobs that fell into his lap was to plan for marketing a new product. The article was already developed, but must go through a testing phase. The job of getting ready to test the product he rated as follows:

Future Value . . . . A

Timeliness of the Work . . . . A

Importance of the Work . . . . A

Since the job rated tops in each respect, he automatically put it into the top third.

The product promised to yield 10% of the company's total sales.

Since the work done on it now would bring benefits mainly in the future, and due to the size of the volume expected from it, he rated the importance of the work as "high ," (A).

If the test indicated that the product was not right, another one would have to be found. The timing of the test was of greatest importance, thus, the A rating in timeliness.

"The greatest value of this simple little rating device," he said, "is that it makes me realize when I tend to neglect the future. When I began this system, I found very few of the jobs thrust at me rated an A on future value, so I knew I was neglecting the future. It's an easy thing to do, but something that an executive cannot afford to do."

Two Timely Questions. The executive and the staff man should always ask these questions about time:
1. *On what work DOES my time go now?*
2. *On what work SHOULD my time be going?*

STRING TOGETHER LITTLE PIECES OF TIME

Do you have one big job, a high value job that you "should get to" but find that you're continually frustrated by present time commitments? Have you considered using "little pieces" of time?

By using little bits of time, strung together, you can get a big and important job done, even if you seem to "have no time for it."

Any big job is only an accumulation of many little jobs. So break that big job down into its elements. You may find that it has 10, 25, or 50 different parts.

By snipping off 10 minutes on Monday, and another 20 minutes on Tuesday . . . and perhaps a half an hour on Wednesday, you can gain many little pieces of time.

You can work on one element of the big job at a time.

You can use small units of time, strung together, to get a major job done.

Here are intervals in which you're likely to find the little pieces of time that normally go by unnoticed:

1. *A few minutes just before lunch*
2. *Twenty minutes just before the office opens*
3. *While you're waiting at a stop light*
4. *Waiting to see someone*
5. *Waiting in a doctor's office or at a filling station*
6. *A few minutes after your office has closed*
7. *While waiting for someone on the telephone.*

You won't get that major job done in a few days this way. It may take weeks, or even months.

But little 20-minute pieces of time, grabbed in small portions each day, can count up, and when strung together, can result in enough time to get a major job accomplished.

If all executives spend all their time on the organization's current problems, who looks ahead? Who will look out for the future of *purchasing . . . of engineering . . .* of *production . . .* of *research* and *sales . . .* or the future of *new products?*

IT TAKES TIME TO READ

Executives and staff men find they have more reading material offered to them than they can digest. Since reading does consume time, a man must choose what he will read.

One executive, concious of the importance of making his time count, spotted one magazine that consistently contained articles that gave him useful information. He had his secretary put it in a separate place on his desk.

She put all other reading matter in a stack labeled "IF TIME." She did glance at the indexes and noted any articles that she should call to her boss' attention.

Even after you choose the one most helpful magazine, you can save time in your reading. Don't read everything in it. Look through the index. Select 3 or 4 articles you feel will help you the most.

FILLING OUT THE TIME AVAILABLE

Time is a form of space. And people tend to use up the space available.

Just as you can put five books compactly on a shelf, using a minimum of space, you can also spread out those five books so that they occupy twice as much space.

So it is with time available and work to be done within that time.

How do you overcome this tendency? The answer: make less space (or time) available.

Do anything you can to create a "sense of time urgency." Set sensible deadlines.

You can set these deadlines for yourself (or for other people). You could break a 10-hour job into one-hour elements. At 9 a.m., after completing the first hourly segment of work, you could set a deadline like this:

I must have phase 2 of this job completed by 10 a.m.

By pressing for the completion of each phase of the work, such as one segment an hour, you'll come closer to using the time available productively.

Without such a device, you'll find that you have no sense of time urgency.

What will happen? The job will take twice as long as it should.

The sense of time urgency comes into play in consulting work. Contrast the time sense of the man who works regularly on his organization's payroll, with that of an outside consultant doing the same work.

The consultant moves swiftly. People in the organization want him to. They know that his office may be charging $25 an hour for his time.

Is the inside man less capable of moving swiftly? No. He *could* move just as swiftly, expending no more than normal energy. But instead, he often moves more leisurely. The reason: he lacks a technique to give himself a sense of time urgency. "

Only You. The initiative for improved use of your time must come from *you. You* must discourage, even forbid, interruptions. *You* must select the work that will count most from the many jobs people shove at you.

CHAPTER 3

THE ART OF LISTENING

We spend about 95% of our time in school developing our reading and writing abilities. We spend only about 5% of our time in developing as speakers and as listeners.

As adults, we usually spend our time like this:

Writing .... 9% *of our time*
Reading .... 16% *of our time*
Talking .... 35% *of our time*
LISTENING .... 40% *of our time*

Obviously any increase in our personal effectiveness as a *listener* must be on a do-it-yourself training basis.

PROVIDE A LISTENING SITUATION

Is effective listening a part of your job? If it is, establish a "listening situation." One executive who listens often uses a special "side-chair" in his office. When it is time to listen, he gets out of his *work* chair, goes around the desk and sits in his *listening* chair. He is opposite the speaker, facing him.

When he sits in this chair he does little talking. He may nod, he may ask an occasional question. He is relaxed and the speaker tends to relax, too.

This man knows that the art of listening is important to his work. So he closes his door and does not permit personal interruptions or incoming telephone calls.

THE "LISTENING CHAIR"

A "prop" like a special chair for listening, can provide a "listening situation."

COMMON OBSTACLES TO LISTENING

Listening is the second half of the communication process. Speaking of course, is the first half. Any of these obstacles can break down the communication process:

☐ 1. *Talking.* You can't "receive" while you're "sending."

☐ 2. *Getting ready to talk* while you're supposed to be listening. (Thinking of what *you're* going to say.)

☐ 3. *Mentally arguing* with the man who is talking. Discipline yourself to hear him through.

☐ 4. *Preoccupation.* Thinking about something else while the speaker is talking.

☐ 5. *Impatience*. Feeling annoyed with the slow pace of the speaker . . . or his inability to get to the point.

☐ 6. *Poor environment*. If you are being distracted by noise, by other people, by things you can see, or if you're in an uncomfortable situation such as a warm room, you won't "receive" effectively.

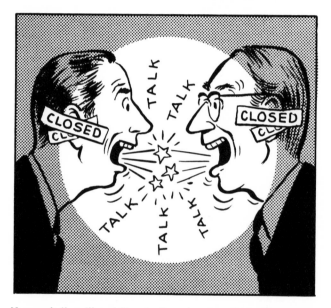

You can't "send" and "receive" at the same time. If two men merely send, there is no communication.

☐ 7. *Divided attention*. If two men can sit across the table from each other without distractions, reception will improve.

☐ 8. *Lack of realization* that listening is not passive. The listener must try to listen. His "work" is to try to absorb what the speaker is saying.

The Art of Listening

☐ 9. *Mental criticism* of poor grammar or of less than perfect appearance.

☐ 10. *Immaturity.* The immature person is not sure of himself so he's anxious to become a talker, not a listener. He wants to tell what he knows.

☐ 11. *Mental or physical fatigue.* Tired? If you are about to listen to someone on an important subject, go wash your face and arms in warm water.

☐ 12. *Failure to see the whole speaker.* Not noticing his expressions, his tone, or his gestures.

☐ 13. *Two senders, no receivers.* Two people talking AT each other at the same time.

DO YOU GET IT? TEST TO FIND OUT

The speaker and the listener both have "roles to play" in the communication process. If you are the listener, you can help insure effective communication by testing. Is your reception accurate?

Test.

After a speaker has talked for a while, ask him a question. Listen carefully to his answer.

If the subject is important, and accuracy is vital, *rephrase* what he said and repeat it, asking:

Is that a correct version?

LISTENING AS A STAFF TOOL

The staff/systems man's job is that of a catalyst. He brings together the thinking of other people, integrating that composite thinking into a workable team play.

Listening is one of his major tools. His main job is to understand and he can understand only if he gets information.

He gets much of his information by *listening* to

As listener, you can insure accuracy. Repeat what you have heard rephrased in your own words.

people.

A skilled listener can be discriminating. As he listens, he can label what he receives, thinking:

This is significant . . . or this is not.

The staff man can't waste his time by letting a speaker go far afield. If he listens with an exact systems cycle in his mind, the systems man knows exactly when the speaker switches to a side track.

Since he concentrates on his *listening* job, he can recognize the path which the line of conversation is taking.

When he knows that the speaker is on a side issue, he can ask a question relating to the cycle's *main flow*. Thus he'll tend to pull the speaker back onto the "main line" again.

EXTRACT KNOWLEDGE BY LISTENING

The people in your organization are rich in experience and in knowledge. Like to put some of that knowledge and experience to use? Do it by listening.

You *can't* absorb information while you're talking. You *can* absorb it while you're listening.

Of course you haven't time to let a man ramble. But by asking questions, you can get the speaker to "make his point."

THE WEALTH OF KNOW-HOW HERE

CAN ONLY BE EXTRACTED HERE

The listener can take a firm hand in directing the course of the conversation. But don't try to control by your own impatience. You can "dry up" your sources of information.

Set limits on the time you can give. Encourage people to summarize what they want to say.

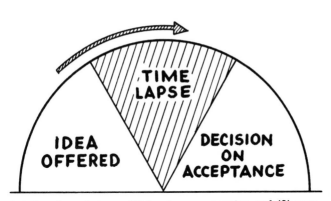

Let time lapse between (1) hearing a suggestion and (2) your decision on whether to accept or reject it.

USE A TIME LAPSE

If a speaker offers you a suggestion, an idea, or knowledge . . . sooner or later you'll (1) accept it or (2) reject it.

If you accept quickly, you may indicate that it isn't worthy of your consideration.

If you reject it at once, you may cut off future offerings of ideas or knowledge.

Use time as a listening aid. Allow some time to lapse before you *reject* or *accept!* This is no place for efficiency.

The time interval may be from a few minutes (during the current conversation) to several days.

If you decide to reject the idea, explain exactly *why*. Thank the speaker for his effort. He *did* make an effort.

PATIENCE CAN PAY

Most of what you listen to will have no value. But *some* of it will.

To improve your listening, adopt the tactics of the

miner in the gold fields. He'd *like* to go up in the ravine and pick up pure gold . . . the isolated nuggets.

But he knows that he must take his gold from the ore that bears it. He grinds it to extract the small portion that is valuable.

You'll already know much of what you hear. Much of it will have no bearing on the subject at hand; or it will be incorrect, inaccurate, critical, or prejudiced.

Yet, intermingled with this large quantity of "ore" will be the small quantity of gold . . . the information you are really listening for . . . that you want to "capture."

SAMPLE YOUR SILENCES

You may feel that you listen often, and speak seldom. But do you? To find out, use the time sampling method.

Take your "talking or listening" samples on a random basis. Six or eight samples a day will do. If, at the time you take a sample, you happen to be on the telephone, note whether you were *listening* or *talking* at that *INSTANT*.

You seek samples of only two types of activities . . . *talking* and *listening.*

Disregard any other samples of your activity. If the sample time falls at a moment when you are writing or reading, disregard that sample.

If you are dictating, don't consider this talking. You are not talking directly to someone. You are really *writing,* using the technique of "voice writing."

After you have taken about 40 samples over 4 or 5 days, how do your totals of each activity compare? Normally you should listen about 50% of the total listening-talking time. What is your score?

If you talked 70% of the time, is this appropriate to your job? A salesman, for example, normally does more talking than a buyer. That is the nature of his work. Yet some skilled salesmen talk less than the buyer.

How do you appear to others? As a talker? Or as a listener?

If you are critical of delivery, you may lose valuable information.

THE LISTENER CAN HELP THE SPEAKER

Some men are poor listeners because they are

critical of *delivery*. Whether the speaker is in front of a group, or is talking to an individual, some listeners think of the method, rather than the message. They think:

My, but this fellow's grammar is atrocious.

OR

Why doesn't he project his voice more.

If you do this, you'll do a poor job of listening. You are not a teacher or a critic. You are a listener. Play *your* role. LISTEN.

Some speakers need encouragement. Often it's a man who is your subordinate. As the listener, you can help. Tell him:

Go right ahead, Jim.

OR ASK

What seems to be the problem?

Look at him. Smile. Wait patiently. If your voice sounds sympathetic, if you sound undisturbed, you'll get the information he wants to give.

If you are not sure of the point he's making, stop him and then quietly say:

I'm sorry, I didn't quite follow you, is this what you mean . . . ?

Use a friendly attitude as a means of getting information from people who communicate poorly.

DON'T BE AFRAID OF SILENCE

The skilled listener uses silence. He isn't afraid of it. He isn't of the school that feels "the air should always be filled with conversation."

After a man asks you a question, you need not give him an immediate answer. You can look at him and say nothing. Your silence is a time for consideration, first of what he has *said to you,* and second, of what you should *say to him.*

The poor listener abhors silence. He thinks about his answer while he listens, and thus he fails to receive. Listen fully and completely . . . and then take time to consider before you answer.

Use periods of silence. Intersperse them in your conversation.

Silence has a receptive power of its own.

Concentrate on the speaker and what he is saying . . .
never on yourself.

Concentrate on the Speaker. The first step to becoming a more effective listener is to recognize the *importance of listening*. The second step is to cultivate *selflessness*.

Center your attention on the speaker's person as well as what he is saying. Don't think about yourself or your problems while you are listening.

LISTENING CAN INDICATE MATURITY

Most top executives have learned to listen. The

mature man knows:

You rarely learn when your mouth is open.

By contrast, the young man, unsure of himself, tends to talk more than he listens. He is anxious to "impress," to let people know how much he knows.

The junior administrator may talk 75% of his total listening-talking time. The top executive is likely to reverse that ratio.

CHAPTER 4

THE SYSTEMS MAN'S RELATIONSHIP

TO HIS ORGANIZATION

What IS an organization?

An organization may be a football team, a theatre guild, a symphony orchestra, the United Nations, or an organization producing and selling a product.

Doesn't your own experience tell you that this is true:

> *It's not natural for people of different skills, talents, and personalities to work together. People tend to be DISORGANIZED when acting as a group, rather than as individuals.*

So football teams must have coaches, theatre guilds must have directors, symphony orchestras must have conductors, and the United Nations must have a secretary-general.

That's also why other types of organizations must have presidents, vice presidents, managers, supervisors, and SYSTEMS MEN. Such people are there to achieve harmonious teamwork, and they do their jobs through:

1. Leadership
2. Influence

Those people can help develop the disorganized but talented individuals into a team if they make clear one "fact of life" . . . *interdependence.*

Interdependence means that each member of the group is dependent on the others for his success. One man is not really successful if the organization is a failure. If the whole effort fails, each man also fails.

Using participation, the systems man can weld together the various work viewpoints into ONE team viewpoint.

GETTING INFORMATION ON WORK

A system is made up of a number of different work operations. The system merely ties these work operations together into a coordinated team arrangement.

To improve the system, you must know what goes

on in each segment of work that is a part of the system. There's no better way of finding out than by asking the man who does the work.

WARNING: This is the point at which the inexperienced systems man often gets into trouble. Don't fence with the man. Be careful how you question his need for information that is now flowing through the system.

To get information on a specific part of the work, ask the expert—the man who does that work.

Ask questions, and let him *tell you* what is needed. Induce in him a spirit of objectivity about the use of information in his job.

The words you use make a difference. The phrase . . . *What do you use this information FOR?* . . . can arouse a defensive attitude in the man-on-the-job.

The same question put another way can get the information you want . . . *Is the information on this form the right information for your work? Does it get here soon enouah?*

PEOPLE LIKE TO BE ASKED

It isn't practical for the bosses to coordinate every move with their employees. But when an employee *is affected* by a proposed change rather directly . . . this is a chance to give the man his "say."

You do take a chance when you ask him about a proposed change that will affect him. He may object. However, if he feels that a decision to go ahead is made only *after consideration* of his objections, then the change will be more acceptable to him.

People know that all their wants cannot be put into effect. But they like to know that they have been considered.

The twin facts of CONSIDERATION and CONSULTATION take much of the sting out of an unwanted change. The result is tacit, if not enthusiastic, support.

This is several degrees better than active opposition or outright sabotage.

There are 3 stages in this matter of handling changes and people.

These stages are summarized by Allan A. Mogensen as the (1) tell 'em stage, the (2) sell 'em stage, and the most effective approach, the (3) consult 'em stage.

Does your organization use the heavy-handed or the effective method?

CONSIDER PEOPLE

A plan that is mathematically efficient is not always acceptable to people. If you have only "engineered" your plan . . . if you have left out all thought of human values . . . you probably have provided a system *that will fall apart!*

40   PERSONAL EFFECTIVENESS

The men and women in your organization have needs of their own. These needs must be fulfilled by your new system.

Of course you also need good engineering in your systems plan. But you don't need it to the exclusion of considering all human needs.

Does your plan provide *more responsibility* for people? Does it make their *jobs more interesting*? Do they feel that it makes their jobs *more secure* or *more important* to the organization? Do they understand *how their own work ties into the big plan!*

The most effective systems plan serves the entire organization . . . the workers, the bosses, the stockholders, and above all the organization's customers and clients.

People don't like to be caught in a purely engineered system,

WORK INFORMATION

Do you tell everyone that systems work has only one objective . . . the cutting of costs? Do you emphasize *cost cutting* to the detriment of the real management job of the system?

The real job of a high-level systems man is to

provide (by working with other people) an effective work communication plan.

If you only cut costs, how do you do it? By eliminating people? Are you a *job eliminator?*

Do you expect people to help you and take part in your systems work if you are the "kiss-of-death" to their jobs and to their security? Do you realize that bosses, as well as the operating people, respect you less if you are merely a cost-cutter?

Do you have the courage to advocate a policy of never firing someone because of the greater production you are able to get through systems work?

Every management needs *good work communication.* Is that what you supply?

If that is badly needed, do you keep running around in the cost-cutting squirrel cage?

If there IS a high-level work communication job to be done in your organization, who will do it if you are blinded by dollar signs over your eyes?

CURING DEPARTMENT MYOPIA

Most men and women in an organization are afflicted with a disease that impairs their vision. It is "department myopia"!

This comes about because of our work *specialization.* We fragment the organization into work-separated groups . . . into departments, divisions, offices, or **sections.** groups.

Each tends to live in a world of its own.

Consider "marketing" work. It uses salesmen, certainly. But marketing is much more. Marketing is the whole job of distribution. It includes *advertising, sale promotion, customer research, competitive research, product development* (based on application needs), *sales analysis, customer services, statistics, profitability of products.*

The successful marketing department does its job. But do the men in marketing really understand other activities? Finance? Purchasing? Warehousing? Production? Tooling? Shipping?

Usually not. Any one department tends to have limited vision.

Rarely will you find someone in the marketing department who really understands the problems of the production man . . . or of the purchasing agent.

So there is both a blessing and a drawback in our organizations:

1. *The blessing:* Men engaged in specialized work become very good at it . . . they're professionals or semi-professionals.
2. *The drawback:* Men lose sight of the importance of organization-wide teamwork.

We have both a plus and a minus value from work specialization.

We want to keep the plus value . . . a high degree of skill in doing a specialized type of work. But we also must do something to minimize department short-sightedness.

The systems man's work is an influence on individuals in all departments. If he first has the team vision himself, he can impart his view to those whose vision is limited by a department wall.

The *systems cycle concept* . . . a principle that ignores department walls . . . . can help him do the job.

The systems man serves as an organization doctor who treats and reduces department myopia.

PREACH SYSTEMS FOR EVERY MAN

The great men of history have been successful because they had a worthwhile message to preach.

You believe in systems work. But do you tell others about systems aims and principles? Do you develop enthusiasm for the work itself? If you do, you're being a man of influence.

If you pound hard enough on the basic principles of systems and do it long enough, eventually your

People within departments tend to have a limited vision of the teamwork plan.

people will become "systems disciples."

Is systems know-how included in your *management development program?* Why not? Get the training men to include it. Some influential systems men conduct regularly scheduled seminars for the management people in the organization . . . perhaps three 20-hour courses a year.

In these sessions they "teach" basic systems principles, which are not only critical to the success of an organization, but which any manager can use.

EXAMPLE: *Carefully teach them the action-memory-report functions of integrated data processing.*

As people in the organization come around to the systems way of thinking, the systems man's job becomes easier. But the important factor is that the systems will be *better!*

So by "teaching" and "preaching" systems principles, the systems man influences his whole organization.

Preach the basics of systems to all within your hearing.

GIVE IT AWAY: IT PAYS

Are you inclined to keep your systems knowledge to yourself? Do you jealously guard your systems principles as "trade secrets"?

The man of influence is a systems teacher as well as a systems doer. The man who hides his systems knowledge can never INFLUENCE OTHER PEOPLE toward better systems.

You are in a position to use a dynamic force. It's right at your fingertips. That force is the "people"

themselves. Teach them at least 4 or 5 of the basic systems principles that you use and you'll increase your effectiveness as a systems man. Then, like the top manager, you're really getting results through people.

CHAPTER 5

SPREAD THE WORK

Are you about to develop a new, better system? Should you share the work?

Don't assume you should do it all. You can use the technique of "spreading out the work."

If you use many hands to lighten the work, you'll have that new system in and producing much faster.

Sound sensible? If it does, the next question is: *Just how do I spread out the work?*

THINK ABOUT YOUR OWN TECHNIQUES

The average staff man, trained in the techniques of systems work, does a good job when he is observing a system in which he is *not involved personally*.

He sees factors about the operation that the supervisor (due to his closeness to the work) does not see.

☞ *But when the systems man is applying his own techniques, he can and often does overlook important factors.*

He fails to see the improvements he could make in his own operating methods.

One of his assumptions is that *he* should do all the work on a systems project.

As a result, the systems man is often burdened with too many projects. He's not afraid to work hard, or to "put in the hours," but that isn't enough.

He's likely to be more effective if he'll just stop to ask:

Could other people give a hand on this project?

If the systems man sees his schedule of projects slipping behind, each getting later and later, he knows the needs are beyond his working capacity.

What does he think of first? INCREASING THE SYSTEMS STAFF!

This is the basic question:

Could I get more done on these projects by spreading the work around?

Have you *inventoried* your own work? And checked your own systems group's skills? Armed with the information you can get by using these two techniques, you can then ask:

What skills COULD be passed on to people who are not trained in systems work?

Often up to 40% of what we call *systems work* can be done by other people with a little training.

> REMEMBER: Many hands are available. If you just work and don't think, are you doing justice to your organization?

If the systems man fails to spread out some of the systems chores, all this amateur and professional help will produce only mediocre results.

THE SYSTEMS LOAD IS BIG

The total hours spent on systems work in an organization is seldom known to the top executives. If they did know the total, it would surprise them.

There are more printed forms to be designed or redesigned than a systems man can handle. There are more procedures that need revision than the procedures writer can do.

There are more survey studies that should be made on clumsy systems than the few professional

Don't try to do everything yourself.

systems people could possibly tackle.

> *And WHEN the larger share of work is done
> without professional guidance, the results are
> poor forms, unreadable procedures, clumsy
> systems plans.*

The number of pros are few. Rarely do you find
more than 1% of the total energies of an organization
devoted to systems work.

Yet the systems work going on all over the place may consume between 2% and 5% of the people-energy available for all work.

Because the need to overhaul systems is so great . . . most administrative people, although untrained in the techniques . . . must and do tackle systems improvement work.

Without the advice or guidance of professionals, they *don't do it well.* Many of the "improvements" are not worthy of the name.

But the effort will go on . . . because it must. The pressure to overcome the drawbacks of poor (natural) systems is always present. Everybody feels it. Key question:

> *Can some of the basic systems techniques be made available to the non-pros?*

THE ART OF GETTING HELP FROM NON-PROS

Are you thinking of ways to spread out systems work? Through this technique, you know you can get more systems improvement work done.

When you use the technique, however, you're assigning elements of systems work to non-pros . . . to amateurs . . . to people who are technically proficient in their *own* fields, but not in systems improvement work.

Amateurs do have their limitations. To use them effectively, consider those limitations. Some techniques have proved effective with volunteers. Others have not. Headquarters people of such organizations as the Boy Scouts, Girl Scouts, Y.M.C.A., and the P.T.A. have learned over the years how to make effective use of volunteers. Here's their advice:

☐ Break the whole job down into parts.
☐ Assign a short, limited job to each volunteer. Test the unit of work. Does it require training? If it does, decide *what* training?

- ☐ If it is not possible to train, assign only jobs that an untrained person can do.
- ☐ Keep the job short enough to be completed in one "sitting." A good unit of measure is a one-hour job.
- ☐ Make the job definite. Remove complexities.
- ☐ Provide a simple set of instructions.
- ☐ Do a bit of informal training by demonstrating how to do the tricky parts of the job.
- ☐ Set a definite deadline for completion of the work—a day or an hour.
- ☐ If feasible, inject the social pleasure of comradeship into the job. Have 2 people working together.
- ☐ Expect and provide for let-downs or failures to perform. Have an alternate volunteer ready to take over. Make all volunteer commitments "public." Publish them on a list, memo, or bulletin, or announce them in a meeting.
- ☐ Make sure each individual knows what job he is to do, and what time he is expected to to finish.
- ☐ IMPORTANT: When the man finishes the unit of work, show *appreciation*. You are the only one who can give him credit. Say his name out loud. Put his name on a "thank you" list. Include it in a bulletin, report, or letter. Give him a copy. Or drop him a note. This is his "pay." It will also assure you of getting work from him in the future.

Not Using the "Know-How" Around You. If you try to make systems improvements based on what you alone know, those improvements will be limited. Your organization and the work it does is complex. It's composed of many delicately balanced and inter-working skills.

One of the strengths of a good systems man is

Break the job down into one-hour units. Give each man one unit to do.

his skill in tapping the know-how around him.

He asks the people who know the work to make suggestions.

These people *are* experts in lines of work such as office layouts, EDP, operations, manuals, forms design, office machines, industrial psychology, transportation, time sampling, work measurement, records management or reports.

Develop a list of people with whom you will have frequent contact. Opposite each name jot down some of the man's work specialties.

Acknowledge any help you get with a word of thanks.

SYSTEMS ANALYSIS AS A STIMULANT

When all his time goes into routine work, a man tends to become listless, bored . . . even apathetic.

Questions asked during a systems study can generate the worker's enthusiasm for improvement.

Yet that same man is *capable* of developing real creative energy. He is ready to accept the stimulation of something new. He'll enthusiastically make changes that *he* thinks should be made.

How can the man who does routine work get a "new look" at his job?

The systems man *can* impart that new viewpoint. He can develop enthusiasm for improvement in all parts of the organization. He can put spice in the daily life of the employee who works *within* the system.

In the wake of a well-conducted systems study, there's always a "mental stirring up." People who haven't thought much about what they are doing begin to ask many fruitful questions.

As one systems generalist said:

> *Often they've made some good changes before I've had time to get back to my office.*

You think people have no enthusiasm for making

necessary changes? Don't fool yourself. Often all it takes is one "trigger" question from the systems man.

USE "AUTHORS" WHO HAVE THE KNOWLEDGE

Do you need a number of job outlines to speed up the training process when you're putting in a new system? Get them with a spread-out technique.

Who knows the job steps better than the worker himself? You can show him how to write the work steps . . . *in sequence.*

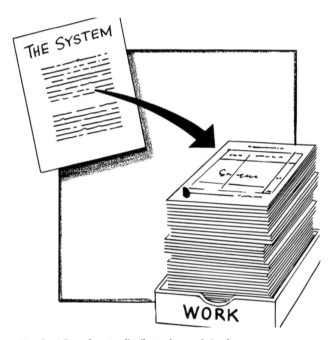

Use the job outline to distribute the work loads over many areas.

Are several people involved? Have them come to a meeting. Then explain the basic techniques of writing a job outline.

You may have to polish their drafts afterward, but such drafts will give you "a fast push" down the road.

Using the man who knows the work is a faster way to get started than to go to each man, interview him, and then write the first drafts yourself.

Provide Back - Up. When using amateurs, people whose prime duty is not the development of better systems, BE PREPARED for their failure to perform. If you've spread the work out widely, you can bet there *will* be some failure.

Train at least 2 people to do the job. Then check carefully. Is the first individual moving? If not, call on the alternate.

SECRETARY OR ASSISTANT?

Many managers do not know how to use the services of their secretary, clerk, or "girl Friday" . . . and most bosses have one.

This girl can help her boss to be a more effective manager. Does yours?

If an important letter comes into the office, does your secretary just drop it on your desk? And then do you have to ask her to bring you the related correspondence and any pertinent papers that may be in the file?

Train her to bring the "complete story" to you the first time.

Do you write short letters that *she* could handle? All you'd have to say is:

Tell him I can't make it in May . . . but will try in September, if he is interested.

The girl can take it from there.

Think out all the possibilities of having your secretary help you by doing a job that *you* now do. Consider anything you do that has a clerical touch to it . . . gathering material, securing information, making phone calls, keeping track of appointments, following up on things due, preparing detailed accounts of your expenses. Can your secretary do it?

She can be more than just a clerk. She *can* be a real assistant, and she'd probably *like* to be!

USE PART - TIME PEOPLE?

The spread-out technique isn't limited to systems *improvement* work. You can also use it as a part of the operational design.

Can you set aside portions of the routine work that can be done by part-timers? Can someone come in for a few hours? This solves overwork or overtime for your "regulars."

The key to any use of persons, including part-timers, is your knowledge of the work portions that *can* be delegated . . . that can be spread out.

CHAPTER 6

THE TEAM APPROACH

If your systems cycle is large and cuts across several functional areas, you can adapt the spread-out technique to form a systems project team made up of line people.

The use of a project team not only spreads the work . . . but also allows you and your systems partners to coordinate your efforts on a group basis.

Use many partners. You may include the internal auditor, a programmer, a data transmission expert, an accountant, a layout man, and several supervisors. Include a systems trainee on the team.

Systems survey on a team basis requires that you know how to make "many people move." It is one of the arts that makes a systems man a professional worker.

THE BIG, BIG SYSTEMS JOB

You have a myriad of systems, large and small, in your organization. There isn't one of them that *couldn't be improved.*

The job of continually improving administrative systems is so big that a small number of professional systems people can't possibly get all the work done.

Most full-time systems men find themselves involved in continuous attempts to improve the major systems . . . *purchasing, manufacturing, engineering, claims, sales, accounting, payrolls.*

But there are dozens, often hundreds, of different systems not so big . . . the smaller inventory systems, filing systems, manual routines of all kinds, contributory systems to the major ones . . . and many systems activities that take place entirely within one department. These rarely get attention with the "intent of improvement."

> *All can stand improvement. Some need it badly.*

There's possibly 10 times more systems work that should be done in an organization than can realistically be done by the professional systems people alone.

Yet the entire systems improvement job should be done if the operations are to be strong, healthy, adaptable, and growing.

But how can it be done?

There's only one way. By getting line participation in the systems improving function.

THE YIELD FROM SUCCESSFUL PARTICIPATION

The results of a successful program of systems improvement participation are many:

☐ *1. The systems man can be more effective in his organization because, with team assistance, he can cover more systems cycles.*

☐ *2. The line supervisor, working with a systems man on a survey team, gains useful education. As he takes part, he makes useful contributions to the new systems plan.*

☐ *3. Any information obtained directly from the supervisor (whose work is a part of the system under study) will be accurate.*

☐ *4. The line supervisor, because he has been personally involved in the systems improvement work, will not resist its installation.*

☐ 5. His work in systems improvement will open the line supervisor's eyes on how his work *REALLY FITS* into the larger teamwork pattern.

☐ 6. Since the line supervisor will, (following work on a major systems improvement program) possess analysis techniques of his own . . . he is almost bound to go on with the improvement process . . . into the smaller systems under his jurisdiction.

☐ 7. The participative process is likely to get passed on. In, improving his own systems cycle, the supervisor is likely to use the same techniques that the systems man used in the larger project.

This will mean the supervisor will involve his own subordinates in making systems improvements. Thus the systems improvement making process reaches the roots of the organization.

With your guidance, your partners can discover for themselves the fun of improving systems. They'll sell themselves on better systems.

When they gather facts about the present system, they'll experience the surprise of discovering what the present system really is. They'll be impressed by the power of their own analysis.

They'll share the mental struggle and then the excitement of redesign. Finally, they'll have the satisfying experience of seeing what they *created as a team* installed and working and GETTING RESULTS!

It's your job to divide the work. *How* you divide it is important. Spell out all of the individual jobs that must be done. Cover the survey, the analysis, and the installation. Then separate the jobs into at least 3 different categories:

Category No. 1. Jobs that only a work expert can

HOW TO SURVEY

FORMS DESIGN

PROCEDURE STRUCTURE

DATA ANALYSIS

CHARTING

COORDINATION

By taking part in systems work, the line supervisor gains new administrative tools.

do. *Example:* programming, time and motion study, linear programming.

Category No. 2. Jobs that the team member from the department can do best. He knows the present practices in his department.

Category No. 3. Jobs that only a systems man should tackle. This may be you or some other professional.

Spread the work around evenly. Don't pile a lot of work on any one person. And then consider:

☞ *Which of the jobs in that list should YOU tackle?*

WORK EXPERT   TEAM MEMBER   SYSTEMS "PRO"

Parcel out the work with great care.

If you don't take that precaution, you may be doing something that the supervisor or the work expert should do. If so, your job, that of tying the team's efforts together, will be neglected.

On a systems improvement project, you're the boss. Apply the techniques of dividing boss and non-boss work.

The effective boss avoids doing that which others can do. He reserves for himself the job that only he can do best. Apply these 2 questions to each job:

1. *Does this tend to string the parts of the systems survey together? Then it's your job.*

2. *Is this job primarily a contribution to one specific part of the systems survey job? Then it's somebody else's job.*

ENLARGING PERSPECTIVE

A man will usually do a better job in his own

A supervisor can gain a larger perspective by seeing how another man's department operates

department if he is able to see how his work fits into the whole process.

One specific way to help him gain a new objectivity toward his own work, and toward the work of others, is to have him study another man's department.

If you have on your survey team, two supervisors who are responsible for different steps within a single systems cycle, let each man look into the work activities of his neighbor as a part of his survey assignment. Tell him:

Sam, we need some information on the use of the systems information as it goes through Joe's area.

Hop over and see him about it.

This role of surveyor opens the supervisor's eyes. He already knows his own work, but this is a rare opportunity for him to see other work that is related to his.

The most significant assignments you can give an operator is to have him get survey information on the segment of work that takes place (1) just before he does his part or (2) right after he has finished his segment of the work.

PROVIDE YOUR TEAM WITH VISION

Most people do not see how their work contributions fit into the entire system.

The man on the job sees only a limited portion of the action. Help him to see more.

Paint for your team members a picture of a winning system. Help them see more of the action than they now see in their work stations. Do this and you will develop "systems buyers."

 You create the best sales situation when your people want to buy the new system.

Are you the systems improvement team chairman? Then you're also a project leader. One of the jobs of a leader is to motivate other people.

Men are intellectual beings with creative minds. Both the leader and the team members can visualize a situation which doesn't yet exist.

When men see something good, they tend to want it.

Take advantage of the human quality of creative imagination.

Beware of assumptions. You may assume that the people within the system now have a clear understanding of the interdependence of work.

They DO NOT have this understanding.

Generate enthusiasm by developing a vision of a good, new system.

USE A PRECONCEIVED ANSWER

Getting people to work as a team is not an easy process.

The experienced systems man will often foresee a logical answer to the problem. *But he will keep it to himself, if he is wise.* Only the amateur systems/staff man clobbers the members of the project team with his ideas of a solution.

The experienced man keeps any such solution

"under the table."

He knows there IS no short cut. The participating people themselves must find out, through their own work, what that solution is.

 The experienced systems man lets the members of the survey team find out the answer for themselves.

But "the answer" can be useful. It can save time during the arrival process.

If you know "the answer," use it only for guidance.

The systems man can use it to ask the right questions . . . to help keep the people from going too far off on tangents . . . to remind them of the really key points at intervals during the discussion.

In short, by having his idea of what the answer probably will be to this problem, the systems man/ chairman of the survey team can steer the group (indirectly) in the direction he knows they must go.

CHOOSE A SYSTEMS AMBASSADOR

The people *in* the system, those doing the work in the departments, must be sold on what you're doing.

One way to accomplish this is to select a team member who'll be a "systems ambassador" in his own department.

Don't accept just anybody to serve on the team. You want to succeed, don't you?

Be aggressive. Find out which man (or woman) in that department knows the work. Is he respected?

One systems pro advises:

> *Shoot high. Ask the department boss himself to serve. He'll probably decline, but then he's more likely to offer you one of his best men.*

When the department head appoints such a man, give him some training in basic systems techniques. Be sure he understands at least:

1. *Forms design*
2. *Procedure writing*
3. *Coordination techniques*
4. *Job outlines and their uses*
5. *Basics of programming*

Then when you have a new procedure to co-ordinate, or a revision to a system ready to check, he can get it approved within his department.

In turn, as he tackles a systems improvement *internal* to his department, he can call on you for advice.

If you establish a friendly, cooperative relation-ship with the department representative, you'll re-spect his knowledge of his department and at the same time develop his enthusiasm for systems improvement work as such.

CREDIT AS A SALES TOOL

In the average organization people are hungry for credit for work that they consider exceptionally well done. A few supervisors are aware of this hunger and satisfy it, but many do not.

This hunger can generate selling power that the systems man can use.

However, there is a right and a wrong way to use credit.

Do you want the credit you give to mean something to the man? Then be sure that credit is fully deserved. Give credit not just for a job done, but for one *well* done.

If you give credit to people who have done nothing beyond their normal duties, they know they don't deserve credit, and your credit will mean nothing.

Consider the qualification: A *job well done.* Doesn't this mean work that is beyond what you'd normally expect?

Has one of the men on the project team done only a perfunctory job? Ignore him when you pass out the credits.

How should you give credit? Tell him? Write it? One systems man advises:

> *Don't tell the man directly that you feel he has done a good job. Do tell his boss. Do it in writing. Make it specific, pointing out how his activity really was above normal.*

He also advises that you don't send a copy of this memo to the individual, explaining:

> *Invariably, the man himself will hear about it, even though he may not read your memo.*

Judicious use of credit tends to put the boss in a buying mood, because the "bouquet" also reflects

Put a "systems ambassador" on your team. Ask for the best
man in the department.

credit on him. After all, he *did* provide that individual for the systems project team, didn't he?

CHAPTER 7

SELLING YOUR WORK

I was working with an executive in his office not long ago, when he took time out to go over a proposed plan with one of his subordinates. This subordinate had brought nothing in writing.

The subordinate was "telling" his boss all about the plan.

I noticed that the subordinate jumped around. First he discussed some of the facts that led him to develop his plan . . . and soon he was off on two or three specific facets of the new plan. Later he dwelt a little on one or two of the "benefits" of the plan . . . and soon he was back to the survey facts again.

He interwove, with all of these other things, some of the current drawbacks . . . some of the problems involved in the present operation.

After a few minutes of listening to this . . . strictly as an observer . . . I was confused. I thought the drawbacks applied to his plan. Then I realized that they didn't, but all was a jumble.

It was also obvious that the executive himself was in the dark and confused. He wasn't even clear about the problem that the subordinate was proposing to solve.

After patiently asking his subordinate a number of questions, and getting answers that didn't clear the picture at all . . . he finally pushed back in his chair and said:

I don't get the picture.

The man with the plan did some more verbal fumbling around, until his boss dismissed him.

Nothing ever came of his plan, I found out later. It certainly seemed to have some good ideas in it here and there, but they were vague. He hadn't been able to pin them down for the man who was going to make a decision.

His boss had asked for a PICTURE. That boss wanted to "see" the plan . . . he wanted to know what the benefits were . . . but the subordinate's verbal presentation alone failed to do the job.

If the man who can say YES or NO asks for a "picture" . . . why not give it to him?

HOW TO CLAIM AN EXECUTIVE'S TIME

The boss' time and attention are scarce commodities. They are not easy to get. When you do get some of his time and attention, don't muff your chance.

Ask yourself:

Which 10 words, written in telegraphic fashion, will most likely grab this man's attention . . . and make him want to read more?

The words that you use in the first paragraph could very well be the lifeline for your plan. If you flub your chance now, your plan and your presentation may go down the drain. All your previous work . . . all your thinking . . . all your gathering of facts, all your good ideas will be gone.

Make your chance count. Don't flub it.

Of course you can't tell the entire story of a complex plan in a few words or on one sheet of paper.

But your main problem is first to get the man's *attention*, and then his *interest*.

Only after that can you develop it. You can develop it by an effective outline, such as:

1. **The situation.**
2. **Probable causes of that situation.**
3. **The short comings and problems you have uncovered.**
4. **What can be done about it.**
5. **What decisions he must make to help you go ahead and do something about it.**

In making his decisions, the boss may want to know a number of things, such as:

1. **How will it affect our organization?**
2. **How will the duties be assigned or re-assigned?**
3. **Has this idea been coordinated with any other executive? Does anyone else agree with the plan?**
4. **If we decide to go ahead, what sequence of steps should we take?**
5. **How long will it take?**
6. **How much will it cost?**
7. **What will we need in the way of equipment, or office space . . . that we don't now have?**
8. **Will we need new skills, or must we develop new skills?**
9. **What is the real objective in doing each of the things that you want us to do?**

HE ALWAYS READS THE TELEGRAM

Take a lesson from the telegram. If you want to be *sure* that your message will be read by the boss, BOIL IT DOWN TO 10 WORDS.

Be sure you have a lot of white space on the paper around those words. Set them in big type. If you do the boss will read them.

By emulating the telegram, you take out insurance . . . insurance that what you say will be read.

But if you insist on giving the man a lecture . . . if you prefer to write 8 or 10 pages . . . your insurance will lapse. When he just looks at the 8 pages, he may scare. He may not even read the first paragraph.

Of course those 10 words can't be about just anything. You have to select and decide. Pick out the one big benefit that you feel certain will interest your boss. Then state that benefit in 10 words. Even if it takes a day to select the benefit and to state it just the way you want to, it's worth it.

Can you take a lesson from the telegram?

THE LAW OF READER RESISTANCE

If you can get it on his desk, the busy executive is likely to read a single sheet of copy . . . if it looks inviting and is typewritten on crisp, white paper.

He is almost certain **not** to read 10, 20, or 50 typewritten pages.

As you increase the pages of your presentation . . . you decrease the chances of getting it *read*.

But, you say, "The man will want to know a lot more than I can put on one sheet of paper. If I don't give him all the facts, I won't get a decision."

You are right. Eventually he needs the complete story, but don't offer that many pages at first. Offer more information *at his request*.

Present your idea on one sheet of paper . . . if at all possible . . . and call for a decision then and there. *Let him request more information.*

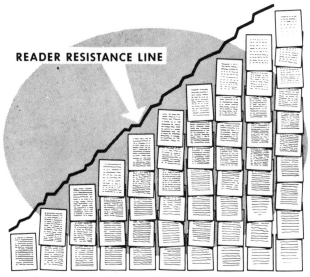

READER RESISTANCE LINE

Beware of increasing reader resistance. Pick the odds that favor you.

A big stack of typewritten sheets scares a man. He says to himself: "Well, there's probably nothing in there worthwhile anyway, and I just don't have time to get at it now."

Make the law of reader resistance work in your favor. On a single sheet of paper type a few words that list the main benefits. This is the way you get *interest.*

USE BEFORE AND AFTER

Experts in the art of presentations have been using the before-and-after technique for hundreds of years . . . and with unvarying success.

Does your plan provide a clear "before" and "after" picture? Does one element of your plan supply this possibility for effective presentation?

The key to the *before-and-after* is contrast. You

can show this contrast by pictures. You can show it by steps . . . many vs. few. You can show it by time differences, by distance differences, or by money differences. Even though the before-and-after technique has been used a million times, it hasn't lost power.

BEFORE   AFTER

EVERYBODY LIKES PICTURES

Can you use a photograph? It isn't always possible, but sometimes it will be. You might want to take the picture yourself . . . and have it enlarged to an 8 x 10 print. Or if you have a photographic service available in the organization, you can get a professional 8 x 10 print.

If a photograph will fit in . . . you can almost bet that any executive will look at three or four photographs.

Subjects for photographs are contrasting sizes of stacks of paper, the condition of a file or a room, the "before-and-after" results of a survey, a layout problem, a crowded condition.

Ask yourself: "Can I picture it?"

You can get attention with a photograph.

Stress the Before and After. There is no sales device better than the old *before and after* technique used by advertisers.

Before, in the old system, there were 745 clerical entries. In your new system there will only be 217 entries. 745 vs. 217. Before and after. White and black. Bad and good.

SELL MORE VALUE, NOT COST CUTTING

Old systems do slow down. They are hampered by

OLD SYSTEM		NEW SYSTEM	
9			9
8			8
7			7
6			6
5	VALUE		5
4		VALUE	4
3	COST		3
2		COST	2
1			1
0			0

Check the value of the present system. It may be necessary to
increase the costs to get the required value.

employee-injected variations, by obsolete methods
and practices, by unnecessary attachments and en-
crustments. All these add up to substantial waste
. . . waste of time, materials, money, and energy.

Some people feel that systems work cuts costs.
Yes, it does that. In a tired, old system you will find
excessive costs.

We are now considering how to best *sell* systems work. Which of these 2 approaches do you think
top management is most likely to buy?

    1. You'll lower the costs of the old system?

                        or

    *2. The new system will do the job better, pro-
       ducing more value?*

Experience shows that management first wants
the system TO DO THE JOB.

We realize that no responsible person is uninterested in lowering costs. We must do so continually if we are to survive as an organization.

But the systems man, if he wants people to *buy* the new system, must first consider the VALUE OF THE SYSTEM.

Systems men have found that their services sell better if they first offer a better system, one with greater value, and then add cost reduction as a plus feature.

What does it profit your organization if you cut the costs in a system that serves your customers when many errors and delays are occurring?

Ask these questions and in this order:

1. *What's included in the present system?*
2. *What is the product, the value, of the present system?*
3. *Is the quality of this product satisfactory?*
4. *How can we achieve that satisfactory product?*
5. *How can we do it at lower cost?*

Costs drop off, indirectly, when you sharpen up the systems flow channel.

UNDERSELL AND PUSH GENTLY

Don't make radical claims for your system, unless you are sure you can back them up . . .

. . . it is wiser to *under*sell rather than *over*sell.

If you think your system is going to save $10,000 a year and you feel that you have enough data to prove this, don't exaggerate. Don't say it will save almost $15,000. It is better to be more conservative.

Say that your figures show it will save $7,855, and then give a little back-up information or "reasons why."

Don't push too hard.

You may be anxious to get your system plan into operation. We can understand this. You've worked long and hard on it. You want to wind it up.

But don't push too hard. Continue to push for decisions, but *push gently*.

Sometimes the best way is to get piecemeal decisions. Maybe one decision first, then another, then still another . . . until you've got them all.

MAKE IT EASY TO DECIDE

Some systems people offer too many alternatives.

Should the new system's key form go on a direct process master, or should it be run on the offset machine? Or should it be processed on an address-ograph plate? Or should it go on tabulating? Or should it be handwritten?

? ? ? ? ?

Don't confuse people with all this.

Shuffle through the many alternatives yourself. Pick out the 2 best. Then make up *your* mind which of these 2 alternatives is best. Then offer the ONE you think is tops.

TOO MANY ALTERNATIVES

MAKE THE DECISION EASY

Keep the alternate up your sleeve . . . in case you need it.

If you make it easy to decide, people will either (1) reject or (2) accept what you offer.

If they reject your first offer, you can offer the alternative.

When proposing a new plan, make benefit-words

a part of the title. So the whole system requires five-days to complete the cycle? Well, let's say that your new system can complete the system cycle in only TWO days. Everyone knows that this is a big step forward. This might be your title—THE TWO-DAY ORDER SYSTEM.

IF YOU ARE TURNED DOWN

If your plan is turned down, find out *why . . . exactly* why.

Executives don't turn down good ideas without some reason. Is some key man against it? Why? Does he lack confidence in you? Or does *he think* it will *hurt him* in some way?

Did you ask the company to risk too much? Did you offer too big a change for them to swallow?

How about timing? Was capital budget low just then?

Are you sure the new systems "picture" was clear? Did you present you new system, point-by-point, with the sales points arranged in decreasing order of interest?

Often a good plan will be turned down, then later, it will suddenly be picked up and installed. *Seldom is good work, good survey, and good analysis completely wasted.*

PRIDE OF AUTHORSHIP

When he sees his proposal torn to shreds, the man new to staff work is often discouraged.

He worked so hard on those drafts, he thought out the plan with such great care . . . and there is his fine work, all torn to bits.

He feels that somehow he has failed. He feels that he should have produced a plan that would be more acceptable to the men who rejected his ideas.

What he doesn't realize is that the proposal was a *springboard . . . and* it served its purpose well . . .

Forget any pride of authorship in doing staff work,

even if it *was* torn to bits.

The old-timer in staff work knows that by the very act of giving another man a chance to tear apart the procedure, or the policy statement, or the plan, . . . that the man has now become involved in that proposal.

Systems work cannot be passive. The systems man must continually press for improvement . . . better systems, better techniques, better machines, and revised policies. He "presses" by his use of the *springboard* proposals.

Selling Your Work

It doesn't matter if his draft is torn to bits. In staff work there is no place for pride of authorship. The job is to develop a final written plan that men will agree to, and on which they will *work together!*

What we seek is action . . . even though the action may not be the same as we originally proposed.

PRINCIPLES OF PRESENTATION

Use these proven principles of effective presentation:

1. Reduce intangibles to concrete ideas . . . like two contrasting stacks of paper.

2. Keep your presentation simple. Be sure that no one can misunderstand you.

3. Use contrast, like the *before* and *after*.

CHAPTER 8

REMEMBER YOUR PEOPLE

You've made the proposal for a new system. The men with yes-or-no authority have said: "Go ahead." You're nearing the finish of your work that started with a survey. But there is one more important step.

Your next step is to *install* the new system.

Installation is a critical time. You'll find that the old system is *more than a procedure* in a manual. It is also a habit-pattern that has become an actual part of the people. Your job is a tough one. It is to change those habit-patterns. This isn't easy.

But if you don't change the old habits, you will find that the details of the old system and the new system will soon become hopelessly entangled.

In some ways you have to "brain-wash" the operating people. You want to get all of the old system out of *their* systems. Then you have to implant the new system and make it a habit-pattern.

Each man must know exactly what his role is in operating the new system. It's best if he also understands the other parts of the system. What happens *before* he does his processing work? What happens *after* he does it? After this learning period . . . after this changing of habits . . . the people will begin to run the new system more smoothly.

Because we have to go through this break-in period, the system advantages will not be realized right away. But they will come, eventually.

ANNOUNCE IT

Just before the BIG DAY, the day you install the new system, prepare an announcement.

Put "selling" in this announcement. Tell everyone *why* the system is being changed. Summarize what everyone will get from the new system.

Get the big boss to sign it.

Have this announcement reach the people who are affected at the right time. Don't send it out so far ahead that they will have forgotten about it when you are ready to install the system. Schedule it.

Tell people when to start.

Yet, be sure that it reaches them soon enough so that they will be ready for any training sessions, and ready to cooperate with you to put the system into effect.

WATCH THE OLD HABITS

Old habits are strong. Installation is a period of habit-changing—so watch the operating people. They may revert to their old-system *habits*.

Some of the people, at least, are likely to jump the track of the new plan and go back to the old, more comfortable way of working.

A mixture of the old and the new system will foul things up generally.

In some places, what appears at first to be an old habit will be resistance . . . or even outright sabotage. You know that dealing with these problems requires delicate handling. The main problem is to recognize resistance or sabotage before much damage is done.

Watch the old habits.

Are error potentials under control? Are people careful on their proofing? Operating people tend to make more errors when they haven't formed the new habits required by the new system.

After the "breaking in" period, the new habit-pattern of the people will become a part of the new system.

WHEN TO LET PEOPLE KNOW

Of course you can't tell people that there will be a new system—that changes will be made—until the boss has said, "Go ahead."

Look at this change from the viewpoint of the employee within the old system. He knows "something has been going on." So he w-o-n-d-e-r-s . . .

Is it going to be bad for me? Or better? (Not likely, he thinks.) What will it do to my job, or my office, or my position? Will I be LAID OFF? Or will I have a less desirable job? Or will I be put into a location that I won't like? Will I be too far away from my friend to meet her at coffee break?

Of course until you had the OK to go ahead, if the employee had asked you about the new system, you couldn't tell him anything. So you probably went about your work rather close-mouthed. Mere conjecture, you knew, might upset him unnecessarily.

So this "just the facts, ma'am" role that you had to play during the study is one thing. What you tell after the "go ahead" nod is different.

It's as though you've reached the top of a steep hill with a sled and now you're ready for the fast ride downhill on the other side.

The danger now is in your habit of being non-committal. That habit may linger too long.

Now you face the job of installation—and *people* must be installed in the new system. So people must enter your plan. Supervisors. Workers. Staffmen.

MOVE FAST. Inform the people, *through their supervisors,* what the new system is.

You're going to need cooperation from the men and women in the present system. Take them into your confidence now. Make them partners in the installation work.

Be sure the employee really "got the word." Some systems men have taken it for granted, that *by informing the supervisor* of the department that he will pass the word on to his people. Don't be sure of that.

Often the first time some employees know about the new system is when it "goes in." There may suddenly appear carpenters, electricians, and painters. The employee in the middle of all of it wonders what is happening. Yet, there has been ample time to inform the employee. It may have been 30 days since the approval, or it may have been 6 months.

A 10-minute explanatory meeting with all employees (held a few days after the approval) can

When you get the approval to go ahead, tell the employee. Don't surprise him on installation day.

Remember Your People

make a tremendous difference in their understanding, and in their cooperation.

Employees often find that they are treated as *outsiders,* not *insiders.* A major change (a merger or sale) may be announced to the public before the employees themselves are informed.

If you want the cooperation of the employee, help him to feel that he IS a part of the organization, not just a pawn in the change that is taking place.

SHOW CONCERN FOR PEOPLE IN THE SYSTEM

When you develop a new system, you know there *will be* changes. The people within the present system know that too, and they are probably fearful of the effect on them.

Often a new system will require less man power than the old one. Or the new system will require a *different* skill than used in the old system.

People know these things—and they are **apprehensive** about them.

Yet, we do want the new system to work well. And WHO will *make* it work? Yep - PEOPLE.

But will they *accept* the change? Will the supervisor be for it? Will the man in the system feel enthusiasm for the new way . . . or will he secretly (or even openly) work for its failure?

If you want reasonable acceptance of the new system, the basic ingredient is:

> ☞ *Real concern for the welfare of the employee who is now doing a job within the old system.*

This concern can't come just from the systems man . . . it must come also from the man's supervisor, and from the general management as well.

Actual and demonstrative concern for the individual within the system will have these results:

1. *A higher degree of acceptance of the change*
2. *Morale will be higher*
3. *If some people are replaced or dislocated, the people who are left in the new system will have less apprehension about their own security*
4. *A general community attitude toward the organization—that it is an outfit that tries to take care of its people.*

If your organization IS concerned, how do you demonstrate this feeling? (Just talk about it alone will never convince the man who feels a threat to his security.) Concern will show if:

☐ 1. *You're making an effort to keep the employee informed on what is happening.*

☐ 2. *You give him early warning when the new system is definitely OK'd. If he must shift skills, you tell him how he can help himself to function in the new system.*

☐ 3. *You let the employee who will NOT BE AFFECTED know that he will not be affected.*

☐ 4. *If a man will be laid off, show him that you take such action seriously and you take it only as a last resort. How about official effort (your employment people can do it) to relocate him in a neighboring organization?*

☐ 5. *Since you anticipate that the new system will use fewer people, you use attrition to help reduce the work force.*

☐ 6. *You keep the regular work force slim by getting temporary help from one of the administrative skills services.*

☐ 7. *You use part-time employees (perhaps 1/2 day call-backs of former employees) during a peak period of change-over during installation.*

You could sum up all of these as:

Doing everything you can to ease the impact of any change on the people. Make this policy a part of your total installation planning.

Lack of concern about the effect of the new system on people can lower its acceptance from those who remain.

MAKE THE TRANSITION SMOOTHLY

The most important part of installing a new system is to make a smooth transition from the old to the new. The work output itself must continue. You can't interrupt it.

When you install a new system, there will be *confusion.* Expect it. There will be *questions.* Anticipate them.

People will tend to depart from the details in the new plan. If it is a good departure, it is a contribution to the plan. If it is a bad one, get those people back on the track.

Control such changes. If a change is to be made in the systems plan, record it. Make it an official part of the written plan.

Consider all possible changes that will come about when you install a new system, including:

. . . *changes in the organization structure*

. . . *shifts of personnel and their skills*

. . . *new physical requirements of the system*

. . . *detailed training and job outlines for the workers within the system*

WHAT DO YOU DO WITH THE OLD SYSTEM?

Are you going to run the old system in parallel to the new one for a while? Or do you think it is best to dump the old system on the same day that you switch over to the new one?

Many systems men feel that it is best to run the old system out, in parallel with the new. They don't think it is worthwhile to change all of the old paper. In this way the old paper can die out slowly.

Is this parallel running of the new system feasible in your plan? Or would it tend to confuse the operating people to the extent that it might threaten the sound operation of the new system? Only you can decide whether a clean cut-over or a parallel operation is best.

INVITE SQUAWKS

Your plan for the new system may be excellent, but when you *install* it, you'll find that there are "bugs" in that system. There's hardly a chance that everything will go smoothly.

In addition to the genuine flaws that will show up in the details of the system, there may be some "magnified bugs," too. These will be created by people who feel that it is a mistake to make the change. They'll use any bug they discover as an argument for abandoning the new plan even before it is installed.

How do you handle them . . . regular bugs and *magnified* bugs?

Screw a sign on the systems door that proclaims SQUAWKS INVITED. The reason?

To get the people who discover flaws to notify you immediately so you can correct them.

Accept each squawk! Definitely invite (in writing) the people who are in the middle of the new system to call your attention to troubles during installation.

The new system will have bugs. Invite squawks from people who discover them.

Get out a letter *from the supervisor* (not from you) saying something like this:

We have a new system. It was developed with your help. The plan itself is OK, but it will probably have some quirks or "bugs" in it. We must straighten these out.

Please be alert. As soon as you see something that should be improved, call Mr. Adams, (the systems man) on extension 481.

DO NOT MAKE CHANGES without notifying me (the supervisor). Reason? A change made at your work station may result in a major dislocation down the line.

Your Supervisor

Don't hide from the unpleasant facts of the detailed boo-boos in the new system. If you do, it could fail.

Don't be thin skinned about criticism. Thank the people who give it to you . . . even though some will come to you in an undiplomatic manner.

Patience. Don't *retort.* Don't *justify.* Don't *argue.* Accept the beef and check it. Admit that you goofed, if you did.

That attitude will tend to insure the success of your new system.

COPE WITH THE LEARNING CURVE

When people first start to deal with the new system . . . their output doesn't increase . . . it *decreases.* Provide for this dip in your planning.

Why? People are accustomed to working in the old way. They've found a set of short-cuts. They are familiar with the routine. They can do the work swiftly.

Now they have to learn over *again.* In the new system, they have to be conscious of every step they take.

When people tackle a new, unfamiliar job, their productivity (output) goes down until they relearn and establish new habits and work paces. Then their productivity will rise—in accordance with the learning curve.

Temporarily, you may need *more* people to get the

work done with the new system. How will you get them? How about an outside service that offers temporary office help?

Or can you recall some ex-employees for part-time work? They're knowledgeable, ready-to-go people. Often women who are now housewives will come back temporarily.

That way, when you are through the learning slow down on the new system, you'll not have a lay-off problem among your regular people.

NEW SKILLS NEEDED? INFORM THE PEOPLE

You surveyed the old system. You know what skills people were using. Are those skills adequate for the new system?

Once you know that there *will* be a new system and there *will be* new skills requirements, inform the people.

To get new skills for the new system, you can:

- ☐ *1. Hire people from the outside who have the the skills*
- ☐ *2. Retrain your present people*
- ☐ *3. "Farm out" the work to service organizations*

Example: Your new system requires the use of a key-punch machine at process point No. 4. The clerk there formerly used a typewriter.

Where will you get the key-punch operator? Can you retrain the clerk who is now at that station?

Can the data processing room furnish one person? Will you hire somebody new? Can you get your personnel and training men to help? Will they find a school that offers key-punch training? Will they notify people where they can get training to fill the new job requirement? Will they do so in time?

Need new skills in the new system? Could present people be retrained?

FADE OUT OF THE PICTURE

Once the system is operating smoothly, fade out of the picture. Have the operator, who has been sending you forms or reports, continue to do so for awhile. But after a couple of weeks you should contact her, and tell her that you don't need them any longer.

WOW! The new system is launched. She's afloat. What next? How about a couple of days off?

"Well," the boss says, "wish we could. But I just had a call. Seems there's a snafu down in receiving, so you'd better.."

CHAPTER 9

THE VALUE OF LEADERSHIP

Does your organization have both *leadership* and management? Or only management?

A man *manages* when he gets work done by directing and controlling the work of other people.

Leadership is something else again. Colonel Lyndall Urwick, world-renowned management researcher, said:

Leadership is essentially a relationship between individuals, the leader and every member of the group he leads.

Leadership, then, is a man-to-man relationship. It is something personal . . . something that you can't show on your organization chart.

Leadership inspires people. It makes them enthusiastic. Plain management cannot "bring people out" the way leadership can.

In many organizations there is little leadership, but plenty of management. The reason? Because the bosses are too busy managing. They spend too large a share of their time on the job of directing and controlling people.

Both management and leadership are essential. If management is the *head* of the organization, leadership is the *heart*.

The people in the organization are little motivated by pure management. They know that it is essential so they tolerate it. They go along. But they want and crave leadership.

When the head men of an organization provide only management; when they completely neglect leadership, you'll find that the morale of the operating people is low.

Since leadership takes time, how can the busy manager have more time . . . time to be a real leader, time so that he can tap the tremendous wealth that lies *within* people?

There is a device that will relieve the boss of much of his management time requirements. It will give him time to develop and exercise his leadership qualities. That device is the *administrative system.*

A system enables the operating people to take on many of the jobs that are done by the executives in the non-systems using firm.

The system incorporates many policy decisions. It provides plans for definite, controllable work channels through which 90% of the day-to-day activity can flow.

The head men . . . if they will use systems to free themselves from the long hours they now devote to pure management . . . can find time to inspire, to improve, to guide, and to decide.

No where is this balance of leadership *and* management more important than in the head man . . . the president or the executive vice-president. The people in the organization want to look up to him, to share his vision and his goals. They want to receive inspiration from him. Executives lower in the organization will not satisfy this basic desire . . . no matter how capable they may be in exercising leadership qualities.

When the big boss has time for leadership . . . when his management job has been lightened enough through the use of systems . . . then he can take a real interest in the people and their work.

He can take the time to walk out on the floor. He can visit with individuals. He can take the time to stop into individual offices. He can show an interest in what a man is doing.

By so doing, he will develop a "feel" for his organization. He will know better how the people at the operating level think.

When the big boss has time for leadership . . . the entire morale climate of the organization can change . . . and for the better.

Systems work itself is not leadership. It is a part of the mechanics of modern management. But the fuller use of such mechanics can supply extra time . . . for the vital function of personal leadership.

**Don't hide in your office. Get out and look at people.
Let them see you.**

PERSONAL EFFECTIVENESS

LEADERSHIP WITHOUT MANAGEMENT

After seeing dozens of organizations overloaded with management and practically without leadership, it is surprising to find a few organizations that have just the opposite problem.

You can find leadership without management. In such cases the morale of the people in the organization will be high, but the organization will fail to get results.

In such an organization there will be no direction. You'll find a complete lack of discipline. While people will work hard, you'll find that they will work on what they want to work . . . and not necessarily on what the team as a whole needs.

In one organization the president did a tremendous job of leadership. He could even tell his employees the bad news . . . and yet they loved him for it. He spent almost none of his time managing and his company was in constant financial trouble.

He was an idea man. He could generate dozens of new ideas, but he lacked the personal discipline to hang on to one of them and see it through until it was a profitable operation before he shot off on another one.

He would assign people to developing one idea, and they would hardly get started on it before he pulled them off and assigned them to something else.

But on leadership he was superlative. He never missed the opportunity of talking to all of his people at least one time each month. He would usually address them at noon time in the company's recreation area.

During one rough spot in the company's progress, a complete lack of work required that the president face the job of laying off some of his people. Inside it "tore him up" . . . and the people sensed that this was so.

The Value of Leadership   **99**

Yet when this man stood up in front of them and told them about the troubles the company faced, and that some of them would probably have to be laid off, he also told them some of the things they could do to keep the troubles to a minimum. He appealed to them not to adopt the practice of stretching out the work on a contract that was closing.

When things did get better, he was the first to stand before his people and tell them the good news before the newspapers, stockholders, or anyone else knew about it.

Yet the entire organization was not effective because, while the company had superb leadership, it lacked management . . . and therefore lacked direction.

Some bosses are such skilled leaders that they can even tell the bad news.

WHAT IS MANAGEMENT?

The word management first meant to train wild horses by hand (for the Roman army). Sometimes we can identify a manager by what he does:

he selects men . . . he plans . . . he makes decisions . . . he evaluates performance . . . he looks ahead . . . he handles emergencies and crises . . . he solves problems . . . he coordinates activities.

A manager is characterized by his holding of conferences, his studies over financial or other reports, his conferring with his subordinates, greeting visitors, considering capital financial requirements and operating financial needs, as well as ways and means of keeping the taxes down.

He may spend some time with his trade associates, with his executive contacts, and in activities that benefit the community.

Of this there is no doubt:

We MUST have management or we will have a lot of untrained, wild horses . . . not an organization.

People understand the need for management. They will accept it and tolerate it. But most people want and crave some leadership, but they seldom get it.

People will readily accept leadership and respond to it. Yet they can look all of their lives for good leadership and never find it.

That's why even a crude form of leadership in an organization will be highly effective . . . if it's combined with a reasonable amount of management.

WHAT IS LEADERSHIP?

Most of us feel a sense of vagueness when someone uses the word LEADERSHIP. This may be because we encounter very little leadership in our organizations.

There doesn't seem to be any school in which a man can learn to be a leader. The prerequisite to learning leadership, or practicing it, is time.

In the special organizations where one or more of the bosses has developed a skill in handling people we can get our answer to *what is leadership*. The basic characteristic of the leader is his concern about the men and women who work in his organization. The great military leaders of the past did not usually have hoards of men behind them, yet they enjoyed the devoted support of their followers. Why?

The men were willing to follow them beyond the duty of the job . . . often at the cost of their own lives.

People will accept management, but they want and crave leadership.

The greatest military leaders ate the same food as their men. They shared the dangers and they shared the discomforts of the men in the ranks.

Certainly a high-up executive is entitled to some privileges that will come with his job. But too many executives get greedy. They want too many privileges. They are proud, and people don't follow proud men.

From the viewpoint of the follower, the leader is a man who never says, *"Do as I say, not as I do!"*

The leader sets an example.

The follower feels that the leader's office is a place to go if he isn't satisfied. That office is a court of last resort if he doesn't think a subordinate leader is treating him justly.

His leader's office, he feels, is a place where his problem will be considered . . . and a place where he can get a FAIR hearing of his grievance. The leader's concern for the worker will be manifested in his attention.

If the executive spends all of his time with other executives . . . planning, making decisions, comparing results, pouring over figures, then he will have no time left to give attention to the people in his organization.

SYSTEMS CAN PROVIDE TIME FOR LEADERSHIP

Since leadership is a powerful force, yet often neglected, getting some of it in the organization is a worthwhile objective. Through leadership the people in the organization will give more effort, more thought, and more of themselves to their work.

The problem of the boss is to *find time* for leadership. His answer lies in two simple steps:

1. *He delegates all non-boss work.*
2. *He uses every systems technique that can help him to manage.*

Systems techniques include the survey and the resultant better system. It includes the job of reducing repeated decisions to one policy statement that he can pass on to the operating people. Then they can make decisions that are at least 90% "on the beam."

Other systems techniques include the development

of action forms . . . the analysis of the work to see if it's set up to reach its objectives . . . the development of better methods and effective teamwork . . . providing a fabric of systems reports that will aid all levels of management.

If he manages through systems, the boss will have time for leadership.

The boss doesn't have to do this himself. He gets a capable systems man. The systems man develops a strong sense of coordination. On any proposed change of policy or procedure, he knows who will probably be affected.

Bosses have a limited amount of energy and time. If the boss uses up his time either in managing, or in a combination effort of managing and doing a lot of non-boss work, he'll have no time for exercising leadership.

But when he does have time for leadership, he can then exercise it. At first he may exercise a rather crude form of leadership. But as he continues to have time, he will learn.

SWALLOW YOUR MEDICINE

One reason management men are loaded with the job of managing is that they will not accept the very disciplines they impose on others.

The president of a small company said:

I don't intend to state my policies. If I do I'm bound by them. I'd rather remain free to make decisions on these matters as they come up.

Yet that man lost many hours everyday because he decided on questions that the operating people could have decided just as well as he did . . . if they had had a definite policy to guide them.

But since the boss would not accept the discipline of one set policy, it was impossible for them to make a decision. With him the answer would be "NO" one day and "YES" the next. He wanted, on the same problem, to go the A-ROUTE ONE DAY AND THE B-ROUTE THE NEXT DAY.

INDEX